at home with ...

The Vikings

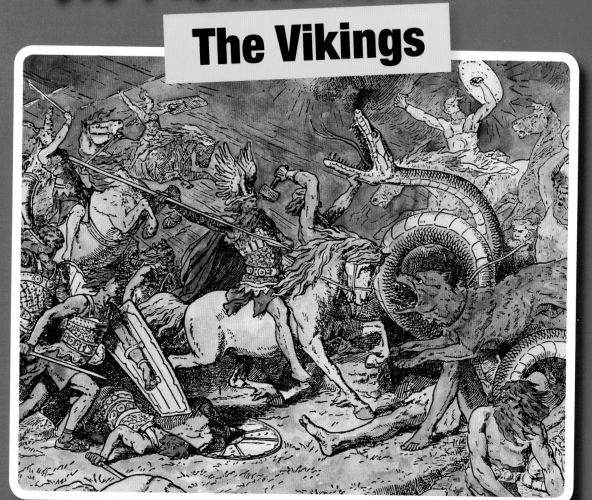

...in history

WAYLAND

WAYLAND

This edition published in 2014 by Wayland

Copyright © 2014 Brown Bear Books Ltd.

Wayland
Hachette Children's Books
338 Euston Road
London NW1 3BH

Wayland Australia
Level 17/207 Kent Street
Sydney, NSW 2000

Brown Bear Books Ltd.
First Floor
9–17 St. Albans Place
London
N1 0NX

Author: Tim Cooke
Designer: Lynne Lennon
Picture manager: Sophie Mortimer
Design manager: Keith Davis
Editorial director: Lindsey Lowe
Children's publisher: Anne O'Daly

ISBN–13: 978 0 7502 8190 4

Printed in China

Wayland is a division of Hachette Children's Books,
an Hachette UK company.
www.hachette.co.uk

Websites

The website addresses (URLs) included in this book were valid at the time of going to press. However, because of the nature of the internet, it is possible that some addresses may have changed, or sites may have changed or closed down since publication. While the author and publisher regret any inconvenience this may cause the readers, no responsibility for any such changes can be accepted by either the author or the publisher.

Picture credits

Contents

It's COLD, **Windy** and **often** DARK
...**What a PERFECT** place to LIVE!

Welcome to the Viking World!

What do you know about the Vikings? Probably that they were great warriors. And that they sailed the oceans on their longships. And that they told great myths. Right?

Well, none of that is WRONG, but it's only PART of the story. We're going to take you behind the scenes.

TOP sailors in Europe!

Hot facts

 The Vikings lived in Scandinavia. This consisted of Sweden, Denmark, and Norway.

 The Vikings became powerful in around 900 C.E. They settled in other parts of Europe, and in Russia and North America.

★ **The Vikings** never had a single country to live in, like the ancient Romans or the Egyptians.

 The word Viking meant 'raiding' in the Viking language, which is known as Old Norse (Norsemen is another name used for the Vikings).

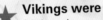 **Vikings were** frightening warriors. They were also great traders and explorers of new lands.

* MOUNTAINS AND SEA! *
The landscape is tough for farmers, but great for sailors!

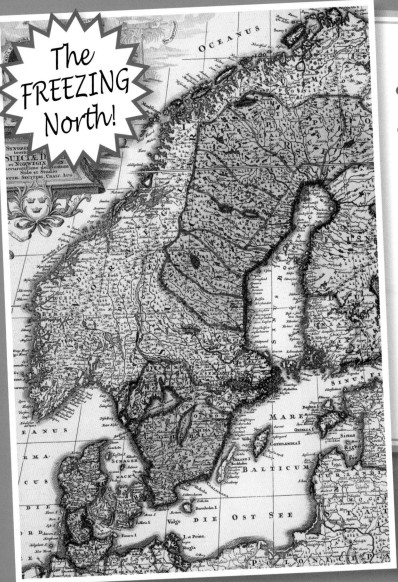

RISE AND FALL

- Viking culture emerged in Scandinavia in about 700.
- After 800, Vikings had settled in Ireland, Russia and England.
- After 800, the Vikings shared England with the Anglo-Saxons. The Vikings ruled the east, called the Danelaw.
- In 911 the Vikings founded Normandy in northern France.
- In 981 the Viking leader Erik the Red discovered Greenland; around 1000 his son, Leif Eriksson, reached North America and founded a settlement.
- In 1016 a Viking ruler, Canute, became king of all England.
- In 1066 the Norwegian king Harald Hardrada died. He was the last Viking ruler, and the Viking age ended.

Farming stock!

Although the Vikings were warriors, most of them spent their time farming. They lived in isolated settlements in the countryside.

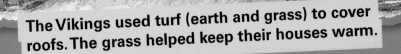

The Vikings used turf (earth and grass) to cover roofs. The grass helped keep their houses warm.

Welcome **to my** Beautiful *Home*

Most of us still live in the countryside, but more adventurous Vikings are moving to towns. Where can you find the best quality of life?

Roof garden
A turf roof means the roots of the grass keep growing in the soil.

* BAGS OF ROOM! *
In a harsh winter, make sure you have room to keep your cows in the house.

A BUYER'S GUIDE

7 Skraeling Street
Denmark DM 728

- Look for a longhouse that is at least 30 metres (100 ft) long.
- Log walls and a turf roof will help keep the house warm in winter.
- Find a main room that features a floor of earth stamped until it is very hard.
- You'll need a central fire with a smoke hole cut in the roof above it.
- Built-in ledges around the walls make good seats, beds or storage.
- You'll need two chests for storage, one wooden bed and chairs with a table.

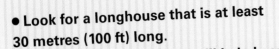

Town vs country **YOU** decide: ✔ **FARMS** are nice and quiet

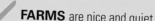

Small settlement
Most of us still live in longhouses with only a handful of neighbours.

builder's Tips

If you're building a new home, there are plenty of materials to choose from. Here's our guide to help you make the best decision.

Stone

✔ Great for lower walls when timber is hard to find. Save any timber for holding up the roof!

✘ Difficult to get out of the ground and heavy to use.

Timber

✔ Tree trunks make good, strong log houses.

✘ Only large trees are suitable. A log roof still needs to be finished with turf for insulation.

Outbuildings

You often see a longhouse surrounded by smaller buildings. They usually include a smithy, or blacksmith's workshop, with a fire for repairing tools. There are buildings for storing grain, and for housing sheep in the winter (it's better than keeping the animals in the longhouse, as we used to). Luxury homes often have a modern bathhouse. Water is poured on white-hot stones to give an invigorating steam bath.

Turf

✔ Easily available. Just cut slabs of soil with the grass still attached. Turf makes great insulation, but…

✘ …it absorbs moisture, so it can sometimes make a house feel colder.

Wattle and daub

✔ Wattle is a frame of woven branches. Daub is the mud that covers it. It's easily available, easy to repair and the best way to waterproof your walls.

✘ Some hardy Vikings use cow dung instead of mud. It can be a bit smelly.

Town or Country?

People are starting to move to towns. They live in small, single-storey homes. And towns are getting bigger. Jorvik in England has about 10,000 people. That's more than most of us would ever see in a lifetime!

 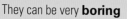

Keep it **in** the Family

Every Viking knows that there's nothing more important than family. Our bonds with our kin are much tighter than with the rest of the community. As for family feuds … once fights start, they never stop!

The HEARTH is at the heart of the Viking house – and family!

Open hearth
Women do the cooking in pots over open fires.

Girl Power

Ladies! Isn't it great being a woman in the Viking world? Have you heard about our sisters in other parts of the world? While they are spinning and weaving, we get to run the household. And when the men are away fighting or trading – which is a lot of the time – we run everything in the village. We also decide when to marry. In other places, women's families decide for them. And, if we get tired of our husbands, we can divorce them. How modern is that?

Choosing a blood brother: ✔ Choose **someone** you RESPECT

SHAKE THOSE KEYS

Keep your treasures in a chest with a big lock and keep the keys on you at all times. If the man of the house goes on a raid, hold a key ceremony. That gives a woman sole charge of the keys. If a husband doesn't return, his wife becomes the owner of the farm.

Boys will be boys

Boys don't stay at home for long, so enjoy their company while you can. By the age of five, they'll be off to live with another family member. It might sound odd, but this is the best way for them to learn to become a good farmer and warrior. It also helps them to toughen up without their parents.

Social **Services**

★ *Has your family been attacked or slaughtered?*

★ *Is someone trying to kill you?*

Erik Shorthair has the answer. Erik is an expert at ending family feuds. Everyone knows how a feud starts. One person murders another, then one of the dead man's relatives kills the murderer. Then one of the murderer's relatives kills the relative. Then another relative kills the murderer's relative ... and so on. This can go on for generations.

DON'T LET IT COME TO THAT.

☎ **Call in Erik Shorthair. He'll listen to both sides and help them reach an agreement.**

(All payments in advance – in case you're killed before I send my bill.)

Blood Brothers Ceremony

Dear Harald Wiseman,

I recently fought the warrior Hjalmar. We've sworn to become friends. What's the best way to do this?

Orvar-Oddr, Norway

Dear Orvar-Oddr,

Try becoming blood brothers. Cut a long strip of turf and use a spear to lift it up in an arch. Cut yourselves under the arch and let your blood mix in the soil. Then replace the turf. Now you'll be sworn to respect each other.

Harald Wiseman

 A feared **WARRIOR** is a **good** choice ✖ Don't choose your **real BROTHER** – you'll find you're already related!

9

Food glorious Food!

We are spoilt for choice when it comes to food, and can grow everything we need. But with the long Scandinavian winters, you have to plan carefully.

Daily bread
Most of our bread is made from rye, barley and oats. It is so gritty it can break your teeth. People who can afford it buy finer, sifted flour. It is imported from the Rhineland in Germany.

Storage cupboard tips

Here are some tips to make sure you've got enough to eat during our long winters.

★ Store meat and fish in salt to preserve it.

★ Another good way to preserve meat or fish is to dry it on racks close to the fire in your longhouse.

★ Smoked trout, salmon and eels are particularly tasty.

★ Make sure you store your supply of skyr (sour milk) properly. Pour it into barrels and half bury them in the ground to keep cool.

Salted fish
Wash salted fish before cooking, or it will taste very salty!

What's on the menu today?

Thank the gods for our cows! We eat their meat and drink their milk, as well as making butter and cheese. Growing oats, barley and rye means we can make delicious porridge and gritty bread. We grow lovely big cabbages, onions, garlic and peas and gather wild berries. They make a good base for adding to meat, fish and eggs.

Viking kitchen **hits** and misses: 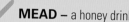 **MEAD** – a honey drink  **HORSE** skewers

A Whale of a Time

Harpooning a whale at sea is not easy. It's also pretty dangerous. So no one really bothers. It is much easier to hunt porpoises and seals, although the meat is not so nice. But finding a beached whale is always a cause for celebration. A whole whale provides meat, blubber and bone for a whole community. The meat is good to eat, and the blubber makes great oil for frying. We can use the bones for carving into tools or jewellery.

All at sea
We hunt whales occasionally, but a small boat against a big whale is a bit dangerous.

Cooking Pots

Cooking pots are made from iron or a soft rock called soapstone. Hang pots over the fire on a strong metal chain from a roof beam. Or you could construct a small iron tripod to hang them from.

It's Party Time!

Who doesn't enjoy a feast? Luckily we have lots, including the big ones after the harvest, at midwinter and at midsummer. If you are putting on a feast, here are some tips to make it go with a swing.

1 ★ Make sure there's lots to drink. Home-brewed beer made from barley and hops, or mead made from honey always go down well.

2 ★ If you can afford it, grape imported from the Rhineland is a very special treat.

3 ★ Give your guests drinking horns. Because you can't put them down, you have to empty them in one gulp. No wonder our parties go with such a swing!

4 ★ Set your trestle table with your very best tableware. Wooden platters and bowls are fine. But if you can afford it, glass or silver cups add a touch of luxury.

5 ★ For cutlery, think metal knives and wooden or horn spoons (no forks – they don't exist yet).

Hollow horn
A horn makes a great beaker – but you can't put it down!

Country LIFE

A year of **Work**

Summer Jobs (May–October):

- **Sowing** and harvesting grain
- **Washing** clothes
- **Bringing** in fuel for the winter
- **Gathering** and preserving food by hunting, fishing or collecting wild plants
- **Making** and mending fences and roads
- **Constructing** or repairing buildings

Winter Jobs (November–April):

- **Spinning** and weaving, and making clothes
- **Threshing** grain for flour
- **Tanning** animal hides to make leather
- **Carrying** wood for fires
- **Metalworking** in the smithy

Don't you hate being typecast as warriors and robbers? What our enemies forget is that we are mainly farmers. Otherwise, why would we always be looking for new lands? We need land to farm, after all!

Everyone knows how tough it is to be a farmer. The soil is not very fertile. The weather is harsh. The summer is very short and the winter is very long. It's so cold and dark on winter days that you can be stuck indoors for days on end.

Where's best for farming?: ✔ **Denmark** ✖ Central **Greenland**

remember the **thing**

Are you going to the Thing? What thing? At midsummer, Vikings in Iceland put two weeks aside to travel to the 'Thing'. It's a gathering where Vikings can vote on different issues (not all Vikings – women and servants can't vote).

The Lower Thing looks after local issues. The Higher Thing, or Althing, is where important decisions and laws are made and disputes are resolved. Some people think the Thing is a sign of democracy (a government in which people have a say).

Mind the **Trolls!**

Everyone knows the countryside is full of spirits. That's why you should never go into the wilderness alone. That's where the creatures known as trolls live. They're old and mean – and they eat people. They are tiny, but if you look at them they become giants. Remember, if you can get them into the sunlight, they will turn to stone.

farming **Times**

Animal League

Cows are the most prized animals. How many cattle a farmer has is the best way to tell how rich he is. Sheep are also valuable. Goats provide milk and meat, but their hair is not as soft or warm as sheep wool.

Raw hide!
Cows are prized for their milk, their meat and their skins.

Going Against the Grain

Growing crops is difficult in Iceland, Norway and northern Sweden. It's cold and the growing season is short. Clearing and ploughing the stony land is hard work. If you have thralls, or servants, get them to do it!

Hired Hands

On the long summer days there are loads of jobs to do outdoors before the nights close in during the winter. You might think about hiring help, as they do in Iceland. But you will have to pay double wages for workers during the short summer.

 **SWEDISH** Coast   **NORTHERN** Norway   **ICELAND**    **Norwegian** Coast

13

First for Fashion

Viking dress is all about keeping warm in winter and cool in summer. Think wool and linen, or imported silk if you are wealthy. Change accessories to keep bang up to date.

Iron working
We Vikings have many excellent smiths, so you'll find great quality jewellery.

Fashion tips for **Men**

★ Tunics are still the on-trend item: wool for the winter and linen for the summer.

★ Some hand-sewn embroidery will make your tunic stand out. Animals and faces are popular designs.

★ Wear your tunic over either tight-fitting or loose woollen trousers.

★ For winter warmth, add a cloak with fur trim and embroidered borders.

★ Complete your look with a wide leather belt and an ornate or plain buckle.

Fashion tips for **Women**

★ Under-dresses are still floor length. Jazz them up with some detail, such as extra pleating on the shoulders.

★ Your over-dress is what everyone will see. It should be shorter than the under-dress – mid-calf length is perfect – and in a contrasting colour.

★ Finish the look with a head-dress made from linen or wool.

★ Make the most of the basic looks by adding a brooch or a string of beads.

★ Try dyeing wool to get different colours. The madder plant makes a vibrant red; use lichens for a rich purple; weld makes a stunning yellow and woad a great blue.

Hemlines Dos and Don'ts: Weave **COLOURFUL TRIM** for your skirts for a magical touch

Stylewatch

Hairy head
Long hair and beards are high style for Vikings this year.

Pouch power
Hang a purse from your belt to carry valuables, like coins or keys.

Taped up
Wind strips of cloth around your lower legs for additional warmth.

Thin cover
Leather shoes slip over your feet. They're thin – but better than going barefoot.

Keeping Warm

Brrrr. Over a long winter, it can get very cold in the far North. It's no wonder we wear lots of skins and fur. No one goes outside in winter without making sure they're fully wrapped up.

★ If you can afford it, line your goatskin shoes with fur.

★ Socks are the latest accessory for keeping your toes toasty. Knit socks to fit each foot. If you can't afford socks, use moss or grass to line your shoes.

Animal skin
Tie your shoes to your feet with leather or hemp laces.

★ Belts pull your clothes around you. That traps air, which helps keep you warm. With no pockets, a belt is good for hanging your knife on if you are a man, or keys and scissors if you are a woman.

Pin it in Place

Who doesn't love a great brooch? Men and women use them to hold their clothes in place – and to show off. Look for highly-decorated gold and silver pin brooches for men, and oval or trefoil (three-leaved) brooches for women. Or check out bronze brooches, which are a much cheaper substitute.

Personal Grooming

Wherever did the idea come from that we Vikings are a dirty bunch who never bathe and don't take care of our appearance? It sounds like a lie made up by those feeble Anglo-Saxons we defeated in England.

Fine teeth
The bone teeth of a comb were very close together to remove lice and nits!

What's that on your chin?

● Vikings are a hairy lot. Long hair, beards and moustaches are always in fashion (for men, we mean). Only thralls have short hair, and who wants to look like a slave?

● A new trend from our settlements in Rus (Russia) is for men to bleach their beards yellow. You can make bleach by using a strong soap made from beechwood ash and goat fat. Sunlight will help keep your hair light.

Viking men often asked their wives to help wash their hair!

tangle free

Hair always looks better when it's combed! There is no excuse for looking scruffy – or for having lice. Fine-toothed combs are made from animal bone or deer antlers. The most expensive are made from imported elephant ivory, although whalebone combs are just as good.

Comb your hair when it is wet. It is more manageable. Married women, make sure your hair is pinned up in a knot. Unmarried women and girls, wear your hair down. Braids are great.

Makeover magic: ✔ Grind up **BERRIES** with mud and animal fat to put colour in your **cheeks**

Stylewatch

A Chain of Beads

To give colour to any outfit, try adding a bead necklace. Orange amber or black jet are popular. To be more exotic, try beads made by mixing liquid coloured glass. It is fiddly work, which is why glass beads are so expensive.

Ample amber
Amber comes in all sorts of yellows and golds. Not bad for fossilised tree resin!

Bung on some *Bling*

When it comes to jewellery, we say the more, the merrier! We have some of history's best metalworkers working today, so it is easy to find great designs.

At the top end are neck rings made from twisted chains of gold, or solid gold arm-rings worn around the bicep. A cheaper option is an arm-ring made out of bronze or pewter. Or why not go for a smaller piece, such as a finger-ring?

Make-up

Feeling a bit pale after the long winter? Crush some berries and mix them with mud and animal fat. That will give instant colour for your cheeks and a ready-made sunblock when the long summer days finally arrive. For a year-round look for both men and women, eye make-up always looks good.

Keep it Clean!

We Vikings are always washing, from our weekly baths to our daily face cleaning. Keeping clean in the summer is always easy. Who doesn't like a wash in a river or stream? But bathhouses make it easy to wash in the winter, too. Stones are heated in a fire until they are white hot, before water is thrown over them. The steam-clean gets the dirt out of the skin. Bathers finish it off with a roll in the snow outside.

Final Touches

Keep your ears clean with the latest 'earspoons'. The best modern designs are highly decorated and look great hanging from your belt. Choose from bone, ivory, silver or other metals. Tweezers make getting rid of any stray ear or nose hairs much easier, and nail cleaners keep your hands looking tip-top.

Earspoon
These are great for getting wax and dirt out of your ears – but don't poke too hard!

Taking **to the** *Water*

If you are new to sailing and the sea, look no further. With our long coasts and our many settlements, we Vikings are Europe's best sailors. We're also the best at building boats, too.

Exploring we will go

Everyone knows the Viking longship. We might be boasting, but it's the best vessel in Europe. It is fast because it is light and narrow. Its keel, or bottom, is very shallow, so it can sail up rivers where the water is only 1 metre (3.2 feet) deep.

Its square sail is made of wool, so the oil in the wool makes it waterproof. Each vessel holds up to 60 men who can row when the wind drops. They sit on the sea chests that hold their belongings and everyone sleeps on the deck.

Square sail
The sail is used when there is enough wind – you'll find it far easier than rowing!

Overlapping planks
The best hulls are made of wooden planks that are bent into shape.

Packing for your journey: ✓ Take your **chest** to sit on ✓ Bring a bowl; you'll need it to wash

That FIGURES

A longship has no front and back. It is shaped the same at both ends. That means the ship can change direction without having to turn around. That's very useful for exploring narrow rivers or sailing among icebergs. Our craftsmen carve elaborate scrolls at each end of the boat. Or they carve a fiery dragon head to scare away our enemies.

Figurehead
A dragon's head at either end of your longship will help strike fear into your enemies.

Dragons were highly dangerous creatures in MYTH!

Import and **Export**

Are you shipping goods to or from abroad? Find a trader you can trust: **Red, Red, Red and Red.**

Use the Best – use
Red, Red, Red and Red

★ We specialise in international trade. That's why we don't cram your goods into overloaded longships. We have our own fleet of knarrs. They are shorter and wider, so they can carry far more chests.

★ **BE AWARE:** All goods shipped at owner's risk. Knarrs are far slower than longships.

★ At your destination, it might be necessary to transfer goods to a smaller boat to navigate rivers. Make sure all your cargo will fit before you ship!

Taking it with you

Ships are so valuable that some people won't be parted from them. They are buried with a ship to use in the next life.

Take that rich lady from Oseberg in Denmark who died recently. She was buried in her ship together with her most useful things. She has furniture, carved wagons and sledges – and a slave girl (it's hard luck for the poor girl!).

Raiders and *Warriors*

We Vikings are proud of our warriors. They are fearless and willing to fight at a moment's notice. No wonder Europeans have been heard to say, 'Save us from the fury of the Northmen'.

Odin turns up at Valhalla on an eight-legged horse!

Which warrior's which?

Warriors don't like to follow the pack! There's no uniform, so they usually wear clothes that are good for travelling. So how can you tell who's who under their leather tunics and woollen socks?

- **The chief or jarl.** Should be easy to recognise from his iron helmet.

- **Ordinary warriors.** You can tell them because they wear leather caps.

- **Nobles.** Elite warriors stand out because of their chain mail. It's too expensive for most warriors. Every iron ring has to be made separately before they are linked together and closed with a rivet.

KILL YOU AGAIN TOMORROW!

Every warrior wants to die in battle and not in bed. Dying in battle ensures that his spirit goes to Valhalla (Viking heaven). He'll be welcomed by Odin (King of the gods) on his eight-legged horse. Warriors fight and kill each other all day there, before they come back to life and go to 'Odin's Hall', where they eat and drink all evening at a feast. Then they do it all over again the next day. And the next. And the next…

Battle **TACTICS:** Slash with your **SWORD**, don't thrust Don't use a single-bladed axe

Making a point!
Steel is made by adding carbon to iron. It's super-sharp.

Tyr
Check out our god of war, Tyr. He's a 'beserker' and crazier than most. He wears a bear's head for a helmet.

Welcome to our... Weapons **Warehouse**

Choose from our huge range – guaranteed axe-proof!

★ We have the very best in swords, axes, spears and bows and arrows.

★ If you can afford it, we recommend one of each.

★ Our weapons may not be cheap, but the swords and axeheads are made of steel – so they last.

★ If you can't afford everything, start with a sword. It's the most useful weapon.

★ Make sure to check out our new range of large, round wooden shields. Each is specially toughened with an iron centre!

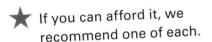
Bargain shields

Let's go **Beserk**

All Viking warriors are scary. But one group is scarier than the rest: the beserkers. They've never shown any mercy to their enemy (they're not even very nice to each other). To get ready for battle they dress in bearskin cloaks and work themselves into a frenzy of screaming and shouting. No wonder they are so scary! And no wonder that to 'go beserk' means to go crazy.

War**lords**

Warriors used to fight in small groups for their families or themselves. More recently they have started to get together in larger groups to fight under a jarl, or warlord.

✓ Use two **HANDS** for your long spear   ✗ Don't **waste arrows** against an enemy wearing chain mail

Trade and Industry

From our trading centres to our workshops, Vikings work hard all over the world. We send our goods far and wide throughout Europe – and to lands beyond.

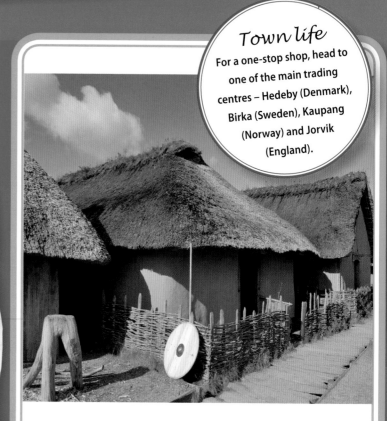

Town life
For a one-stop shop, head to one of the main trading centres – Hedeby (Denmark), Birka (Sweden), Kaupang (Norway) and Jorvik (England).

JARL, KARL OR THRALL?

Dear Harald Wiseman,
I'm a bit confused. I keep hearing men described as jarls, karls or thralls. It's important, because it decides what job we do. What's the difference?

Yours,

Grettir Eriksson

Dear Grettir,
That's a good question. These are three positions in society. A jarl is a ruler or warlord. A karl is a freeman. And a thrall is a slave.

Karls do most of the jobs. But some poor karls become thralls in return for food and shelter. But thralls have no rights and have to do horrible jobs no one else wants.

Yours, Harald Wiseman

A TRADING WE WILL GO

Our merchants sail wherever they can do business. The Swedes have made it as far as Byzantium (now Istanbul), the heart of the Byzantine Empire, and to Jerusalem in the eastern Mediterranean. Other traders have headed west to Britain and beyond.

These traders are a clever bunch. Many of them are becoming Christians so they can trade more easily with Christian countries. They wear the Christian cross next to the hammer, the symbol of our god Thor.

Rules for **trade:** ✔ Make sure **passengers pay** for a voyage – in goods if possible

Imports and Exports

Viking **merchants** can get you almost **anything** – and can **sell** almost anything **overseas**.

Leave my tusks alone!

VIKING STORES

Get the latest from Scandinavia!

- AMBER. This fossilised tree resin makes great jewellery.

- FURS AND SKINS. They make the warmest clothes.

- WHALE AND SEAL SKIN. Make great waterproof ropes.

- IVORY. Walrus ivory is carved into jewellery.

- TIMBER. Great for building houses and ships.

- IRON. Popular for making weapons and tools!

Bartering

Bartering is still the most popular means of exchanging goods but silver coins are being used more often as money since King Harald Bluetooth ordered lots to be made.

VIKING STORES

Goods from around the world – all in ONE PLACE!

- SILVER. We used to get it from Arabia, but try silver from Germany and Britain.

- SALT. From the Mediterranean. Essential for preserving food for winter.

- GLASS. From France, glass is on everyone's wish list for drinking cups and jewellery.

- SLAVES. There's high demand for slaves from the Baltic Sea.

- SILK AND SPICES. They're not cheap – but they come all the way from East Asia.

Timber!
Fir trees from our forest produce long, straight wood to use for building.

❌ **DON'T RUSH** a voyage to Iceland. Sail there one summer and return the next ✔ Take lots of silver coins for trade

23

A Handy Guide for Tourists

'Have boat, will travel'. That pretty much sums up us Vikings. But where are the best places to go these days?

STAR RATING

✸✸✸✸✸ Unmissable
✸✸✸✸ Worth a detour
✸✸✸ Visit if you are in the neighbourhood
✸✸ Don't bother
✸ Stay at home

Name changer!
So many Norsemen settled in northern France the region was renamed Normandy.

Russia

Currently the number one destination for Vikings from Sweden. They control Kiev and Novgorod and have named the region Rus. From there, they can travel along the River Dnieper towards the Black Sea and the trade routes of the Byzantine Empire. Trading is so profitable that there are Viking settlements everywhere in Rus.

Normandy

When we Vikings tried to capture Paris, we failed. But never mind. Normandy has been a good substitute for Viking settlements in France. The rumour is that our men are settling permanently in this outpost of northern France. They marry local women and call themselves Norsemen, or Normans. Whatever next?

Also **worth** a **look:** Novgorod, capital of **RUS** **Byzantium**, capital of the Byzantine Empire

Greenland

Greenland is a long way to go – it's beyond Iceland – and you'll find that it is definitely not green. This is an icy wasteland.

Blame Erik the Red. When he got to Greenland, he knew no other Viking would be silly enough to live there unless he gave it an attractive name. It's a good place for polar bear skins and walrus ivory – and not much else!

Turf houses
The Viking settlement at L'Anse aux Meadows in Canada was soon abandoned.

North America

Another one to avoid. Leif 'the Lucky' Eriksson, the son of Erik the Red, sailed beyond Greenland. He gets 10/10 for bravery but things have been tough for Vikings in 'Newfoundland' ever since. Scary Native Americans live there. These 'skraelings' are as tough as us, and they like a fight. So for the time being, North America is best left off the tourist trail.

England

This is a winner. It is close by and those Anglo-Saxons are a feeble bunch. We've had lots of successful raids and we control at least half of the country. What's more, those English hand over gold and silver in return for peace. When we asked them for a ransom – called Danegeld – of £10,000, they paid up at once!

The first Viking RAID in England was on Lindisfarne Island.

One to **AVOID**: The **WHITE SEA** – it's too cold, even for us!

PASSING the Time

We Vikings aren't always travelling, fighting or farming. We also like to have fun! There are loads of things to do all year round, so take your pick!

Full speed ahead
Sledges were useful for dragging loads, not just for having fun!

WINTER Sports

The winter is not **all bad.** There are great **outdoor sports** to enjoy in the daylight, and **board games** for indoors.

Board Games

If winter sports sound too energetic, stay inside by the fire and play board games. One favourite is 'hnefatafl'.

HOW TO PLAY
The game is played on a square board. One player has the 'king', who starts in the middle and has to get to a corner square. The king is defended by eight 'soldiers'. The other player has 16 soldiers and has to use them to try to capture the king.

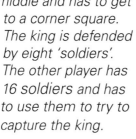

Snow and **Ice!**

Get out your skis and sledges. There's sledging, skiing and ice-skating. Skates are easy to make. Scrape animal bones until they are straight and smooth. Then tie them to your shoes with straps of leather and off you go. Skis are bigger versions of skates, and sledges are just like two large skis under a wooden frame.

A Viking's **GYM** bag: Ice-skates **SWIMMING** costume Rawhide **ROPES**

SUMMER Sports

There's a lot **to do** to fill the **long summer days**. There are running and rowing games, swimming, ball games and a **competition** called throwing the boulder (you can probably **work out what** that's all about!).

Fab feasts!

A feast is a great time to get together with your family and friends. Check out where you are sitting. The most important guests are near the host, who sits in the high chair at the head of the table. If you are by the door, you aren't very important!

Tug-of-WAR

Rawhide rope
Viking ropes were made from cow leather or whale or walrus skin.

This is always a popular test of strength. Two teams pull either end of a long rope to try to drag the other team over a dividing line. A fun variation is the skin game. Two opponents pull on an animal skin until one falls and lets go – or until the skin splits.

Wrestling
Some Viking warriors are expert wrestlers. They use their legs more than their arms to pin down their opponents.

Horse Fighting

This is a favourite pastime in Iceland. It's much more popular than horse racing. Two prized stallions fight to the death using their teeth and hooves. People bet on which horse might win. We Vikings believe that horses are sacred animals, so we often hold horse fights during religious feasts and ceremonies.

With a set of gnashers like these, I can hold my own against anyone!

Are you sitting **Comfortably?**

Who doesn't love a good saga? Sitting around the fire listening to stories about gods and goddesses passes many a winter night.

Our poets are called skalds. They know lots of poems off by heart. They need to, because none of them are written down (although they might be in the future). But they can also make up new poems at a moment's notice if asked by the host of a feast. Remember how Egil Skallagrimsson, the famous skald, saved his life by making up a poem to celebrate the courage of an enemy?
It was called
Egil's Saga.

Ragnarök
The giant wolf Fenrir will fight at Ragnarök and will kill Odin, king of the gods.

Goodies & **baddies:** ✔ **Odin,** king of the gods ✔ **Frigg,** wife of **ODIN** ✖ **Fenrir** the **WOLF**

LOKI'S MYTH

Loki is the god of mischief. We all have a soft spot for him, although he causes trouble. One of Loki's wives was the giantess Angroboda. Loki turned himself into a female horse and ran off with Angroboda's horse. He gave birth to an eight-legged foal named Sleipnir. He gave the horse to Odin, who used it as his magical steed.

Giant killer
Thor, god of thunder, leads the gods' fight against the giants.

FREYA'S MYTH

Freya is the goddess of beauty, love and jewellery. As you might guess, she likes nice things!

Freya owned a beautiful necklace named Brisingamen. Odin got Loki to steal it, then told Freya she could only have it back if she became the goddess of war. Freya agreed. From then on, half the warriors killed in battle went to stay with her and the rest went to stay with Odin in Valhalla.

Myth of **Thor**

Thor was only parted from his magic hammer, Mjölnir, once. The giant Thrym stole Mjölnir and said he would only return it if the goddess, Freya, became his wife. Thor agreed, but turned up at the wedding disguised as Freya. Thrym placed the hammer on the knee of what he thought was his new wife. Thor grabbed it, and killed Thrym and all the wedding guests. He was never parted from his hammer again!

Magical Myths
Even though Odin is our most important god, Thor is everyone's favourite. What he lacks in brains he makes up for in brawn. He never goes anywhere without his magic hammer, Mjölnir.

Glossary

amber A gold or yellow fossil formed from the resin of ancient trees.

bartering Trading by exchanging goods for other goods, not money.

blubber A layer of fat that helps insulate sea mammals such as whales.

brooch An ornament that is pinned onto a piece of clothing.

earspoon A long, small scoop that is used to clean out the ears.

embroidery Using a needle and thread to decorate a piece of cloth.

feud A long and bitter quarrel between members of two families.

figurehead A carving at the front of an old-fashioned sailing boat.

insulate To use a layer of material to help keep something or someone warm.

jet A hard, black stone that can be polished to a shine.

knarr A broad, slow wooden boat used by the Vikings for trade.

longhouse A large, single-roomed dwelling for a whole family.

longship A long, narrow ship powered by sails or by rowers.

mead An alcoholic drink made from fermented honey and water.

ransom A sum of money demanded in return for something.

skald A poet who told stories about Viking heroes and their deeds.

skraeling A native inhabitant of North America during Viking settlement.

smith A person who works by shaping metal over a white-hot fire.

trestle A table supported by detachable legs.

tunic A loose, sleeveless garment that reaches to the knees.

turf A piece of earth held together by the roots of the grass growing in it.

On the web

http://www.bbc.co.uk/schools/primaryhistory/vikings/
BBC schools site all about the Vikings and their lives.

http://www.bbc.co.uk/history/ancient/vikings/
Another BBC site, with more information about the Vikings.

http://jorvik-viking-centre.co.uk/who-were-the-vikings/
A guide from the Viking Centre in the old Viking town of Jorvik (York).

http://www.britishmuseum.org/explore/cultures/europe/vikings.aspx
An introduction to the Vikings from the British Museum, including a gallery of artifacts.

Books

Anderson, Peter. *Vikings* (History's Greatest Warriors). Torque Books, 2011.

Boyer Binns, Tristan. *On to Valhalla! The Vikings* (Fusion). Raintree, 2007.

Butterfield, Moira. *The Vikings in Britain* (Tracking Down). Franklin Watts, 2013.

Cox, Michael. *10 Best Viking Legends Ever*. Scholastic, 2009.

Deary, Terry. *The Vicious Vikings* (Horrible Histories). Scholastic, 2007.

Harman, Alice. *The Vikings* (The History Detective Investigates). Wayland, 2014.

McDonald, Fiona. *Vikings* (100 Facts). Miles Kelly Publishing Ltd., 2008.

Margeson, Susan M., and Peter Anderson. *Viking* (Eyewitness). Dorling Kindersley, 2005.

Powell, Jillian. *The Vikings* (Gruesome Truth About). Wayland Books, 2010.

Wingate, Philippa. *Viking World* (Usborne Illustrated World History). Usborne Publishing Ltd, 2013.

Index